Lil' Margaret, *an F6-D, takes off. The F-6D was the photoreconnaissance version of the P-51D. Original P-51D production plans called for more than 200 F-6Ds, but by the fall of 1944 the pressure for fighters forced cutbacks in recon conversion. Eventually 136 P-51Ds were converted into F-6Ds and 163 P-51Ks were converted into F-6Ks, another photoreconnaissance aircraft.*

Designed by Dan Patterson. Edited by Katherine A. Neale and Ross A. Howell, Jr.

Library of Congress Catalog Card Number 95-75501

ISBN 0-943231-75-2

Printed in Hong Kong.

Published by Howell Press, Inc. 1147 River Road, Suite 2, Charlottesville, VA 22901, Telephone 804-977-4006

First printing

HOWELL PRESS

Previous page: Some of the personal equipment associated with the crews who flew and serviced the P-51 Mustang. From left: a mechanic's fleece-lined D-1 jacket and coveralls; a blue star flag hung in the windows by the families back home in the United States (if a loved one was killed in action the family hung a flag with a gold star); stationery for those important letters home; the North American Aviation flight manual for the P-51; an RAF flight helmet and goggles, an oxygen mask and leather gloves, the "hack" watch which was important for timing at takeoff, rendezvous, and return to base; the pilot's information file which contains basic information about flying for the USAAF. Far right, the pilot's leather A-2 jacket. Bottom right, the pilot's maps and simple navigational tools.

Preface

The P-51 Mustang was the premier propeller-driven fighter of World War II. These airplanes and the men who flew them changed the face of the air war over Europe. The Mustang, with its superior engine, superior firepower, and long range, protected the bombers, took the war to the Luftwaffe, and defeated it.

This book is the first in our "Living History" series to have a fighter as its subject. A single-engine, single-seat fighter presents an interesting set of problems for a photographer: could I put the reader in the pilot's seat and into the shoes of the ground crews who kept them flying?

The sound of the Mustang's Merlin engine is one of the most recognizable icons of the World War II era. The only thing better than hearing one is to hear several — on the deck — going flat out.

Dan Patterson
March 7, 1995

USAFM

MUSTANG

North American P-51

Photographs by Dan Patterson
Text by Paul Perkins

MUSTANG

Though generally regarded as the premier American fighter plane to emerge from World War II, the P-51 Mustang owes both its origin and its most important performance development to the British. As 1940 approached, the British aircraft industry was working around the clock to supply Royal Air Force (RAF) squadrons who would defend the British Isles. The German war machine was poised to unleash a blitzkrieg on western Europe. England's interests in the Middle East and Far East could not be protected without purchasing modern fighters and bombers from the United States.

The British Purchasing Commission (BPC) was instructed to acquire a fighter that

Schmued, NAA's chief designer, were convinced NAA could design and build an airplane that was better than the Curtiss P-40. Schmued created a proposal for Kindelberger to take to England that included an inboard profile, a three-view drawing, performance and weight estimates, specifications, and some detailed drawings of the armament.

Schmued's proposed plane was the fastest that could be built around a 5'10", 140-pound man. The armament consisted of two 20-millimeter cannons in each wing. The airframe met the design strength requirements of the USAAC.

Dutch Kindelberger returned without a contract, but he was confident enough to

amples of Model NA-73 (as it was then known). A formal contract detailing terms, conditions, quantity (300), and schedule was signed on May 23, 1940, and the prototype completion date was estimated for January 1941.

A herculean effort was required to get the airplane designed and constructed in accordance with that schedule. Sixteen-hour workdays were the norm. North American's preliminary design group consisted of experienced designers who were familiar with the latest innovations in structural materials and in the concepts of engines and cooling, aerodynamics, propellers, and a host of other technological advances. Raymond H. Rice was chief engi-

North American XP-51.

"One afternoon in March, Dutch Kindelberger came to my office and said, 'Ed, do we want to build P-40s here?' From the tone of his voice, I knew what kind of answer he expected. I said, 'Well, Dutch, don't let us build an obsolete airplane, let's design a better one and build a better one.'"
— Edgar Schmued, Chief designer, North American Aviation

would perform well in ground attack missions. The British liked the Curtiss P-40 Tomahawk, but Curtiss was already having problems meeting the United States Army Air Corps' (USAAC) demand for P-40s. The USAAC had ordered the XP-46, successor to the P-40, on September 29, 1939, and there was no way production of the P-40 would be interrupted for the introduction of a new fighter plane.

On February 25, 1940, the BPC approached James "Dutch" Kindelberger, president of North American Aviation (NAA), with the suggestion that the BPC sub-contract NAA to build Curtiss P-40s. Dutch Kindelberger was not interested.

Both Kindelberger and Edgar

order a mock-up built. On April 11, 1940, about two weeks after Kindelberger had returned to the United States, the British sent NAA a letter of intent for the purchase of 400 North American "N.A.-50B" single-seat fighters. The proposed plane was to have an Allison engine and its unit cost was not to exceed $40,000.

On April 24, 1940, company general order NA-73 was issued for the construction of one "Allison-engined pursuit." The Mustang was born.

On May 4, 1940, NAA signed a foreign release agreement with the USAAC for sale of the fourth and tenth production ex-

neer. Edgar Schmued, the chief designer, was destined to be known as "Mr. Mustang."

As was the case with the B-24 Liberator, the magic of the NA-73 was in the design of the wings. The National Advisory Committee for Aeronautics (NACA) – whose functions were transferred to NASA in 1958 – had been conducting wind tunnel research at Langley, Virginia. In June 1939 NACA published the results of its studies regarding laminar flow airfoils. The laminar flow wing design reduced the drag caused by airflow turbulence over the wing surface. Turbulence in the boundary layer — the region of retarded airflow immediately adjacent the wing surface — typically began to occur very close to the wing's leading edge. Using a laminar flow airfoil to delay the onset of this turbulence to a point further aft on the wing resulted in less induced drag. Less induced drag meant greater speed.

Ed Horkey, a young aerodynamicist, and his design team were just two months along in the creation of the NA-73 when they teamed up with engineers from NACA to determine the best wing plan for the NA-73. In a world without computers, this meant a small army of technicians crunching through hundreds of thousands of numbers with electric calculators. They ran wind tunnel tests at North American, the California Institute of Technology, and the University of Washington.

Sq/Leader C.E. Stout, Number 414 Squadron RCAF, Mustang I. Collection of Clyde East

These tests led to several decisions concerning the design of the NA-73. The undercarriage and flaps were operated hydraulically. Both the oil and glycol radiators were placed below and behind the cockpit area inside a carefully designed duct, which was streamlined and faired into the fuselage. The duct was fitted with its own retractable air scoop and an opening gate aft of the radiator. Theoretically the drag the duct added should have been partially compensated for by cool air traversing the radiators, expanding in volume as it was warmed, and exiting aft as thrust. This turned out to be more of a theoretical advantage than a practical reality. Unfortunately, the plumbing required

to move coolant to and from the engine would prove vulnerable to ground fire.

Everything from the firewall forward, including the engine installation, was designed by an air racing pilot named Art Chester. The engine initially chosen for the Mustang was the Allison V-1710-F36, the most powerful in-line engine produced in the United States at that time. This V-12 engine was rated at 1,150 horsepower at 11,800 feet, allowing the Mustang to perform best at low to medium altitudes.

The British Air Ministry requirement had initially specified that the Mustang have an eight-gun armament similar to that of British Spitfires and Hurricanes. The North American designers suggested an armament of either four 20-millimeter cannons or two .50-caliber and two .30-caliber weapons. The decision must have been left to a committee because the design for the NA-73 called for an odd mix of eight guns. There were two .50-caliber Browning MG 53s in the fuselage astride the engine crankcase with synchronizers to allow firing through the propeller arc. Each wing carried one .50-caliber MG 53 and a pair of .30-caliber MG 40s, all of which fired outside the propeller arc. The windscreen was bulletproof and the pilot was protected by armor plate behind his seat.

The design and construction of the NA-73 progressed rapidly; the basic prototype airframe was completed in 102 days. After the prototype was rolled out, technicians waited eighteen days for an Allison engine. The prototype NA-73X flew from Mines Field, California, on October 26, 1940 — more than a year before the United States would enter World War II. By this time, the BPC had already placed a second order for an additional 320 aircraft. On the fifth test flight, the pilot ran one of the fuel tanks dry, failed to switch over to another tank, and crashed in a plowed field, severely damaging the plane. The crash was no fault of the design. The performance of the NA-73X was so good, and the need of the British was so great, that the program was never in danger.

The British were not only the first to place an order for the NA-73, they were also the ones who named it. In a letter to North American dated December 9, 1940, the BPC stated: "We are to inform you that the above mentioned airplanes (contract NA-73) are to be given the official designation 'Mustang' and this name shall be used in all correspondence."

Two Mustang production aircraft were appropriated by the United States Army Air Force (USAAF) for testing at Wright Field, Dayton, Ohio. The USAAF designated these aircraft XP-51. When the first XP-51 arrived at Wright Field on August 24, 1941, it was assigned a low priority. This low priority status, and bad weather, delayed official testing until October 6, 1941. When the USAAF Pursuit Board met October 11-30, 1941, to discuss the ongoing program for pursuit aircraft development, the XP-51 was not mentioned. The USAAF felt it had an abundance of choices without having to consider the XP-51. In any case, the Mustang had not been built to meet USAAC or USAAF specifications; it had been created for the RAF.

The Mustang was impressive in its USAAF tests. The fighter had a top speed of 382 MPH at 13,000 feet, which exceeded the 375 MPH guaranteed by NAA. The Mustang's range was 750 miles at a cruising speed of 325

P-51A on the deck.

USAFM

MPH. The Mustang maneuvered better than any of its contemporaries, except the Vultee P-66. The Mustang's laminar flow wing design had a higher critical Mach number than the older NACA airfoil designs on the P-38 and P-39. This meant that the Mustang pilot could break off combat by diving away at much higher speeds than his adversary could match.

The first production Mustang I arrived in Great Britain on October 21, 1941, and was first flown less than a month before the United States was drawn into World War II by Japan's surprise attack on Pearl Harbor on December 7, 1941. The British were very enthusiastic about the Mustang's handling and cockpit layout. Only minor modifications were deemed necessary. The RAF found the Mustang to be an excellent low- and medium-altitude fighter. It was certainly the best American fighter available to the RAF at that time. Comparisons made between the maneuverability of the Spitfire VB and the Mustang I at regular combat loads revealed that below 25,000 feet, the Spitfire outmaneuvered the Mustang. The Spitfire could turn inside and outclimb the Mustang, but the Mustang dove faster and had greater speed in level flight: 382 MPH at 15,000 feet. Though the latter advantage didn't mean much for fighter squadrons, which typically operated above 15,000 feet, the British felt the Mustang was an ideal replacement for the Westland Lysanders and Curtiss P-40 Tomahawks which the RAF Army Co-operation Command was then using.

Number 26 Squadron RAF received the Mustang I in February 1942 and made the first operational sortie over the French coast on May 5, 1942.

By July 1942 the RAF was using Mustangs in daylight low-altitude photoreconnaissance missions called "Rangers." The fighters on these camera missions were equipped with a single K-24 camera, positioned behind the pilot. The camera was pointed downward and backward, allowing the pilot to photograph objects on the ground as they passed to his left.

The British also used the Mustang I and II for daylight intrusion raids over the continent. These missions were called "Rhubarbs." The Allison, unlike the later Merlin engines, ran very smoothly at low RPM, allowing the British to obtain remarkably low fuel consumption and giving them an operational range greater than that of any other fighter they possessed.

The cruise to the coast was flown at 200 KIAS (knots indicated air speed) and 1,100 RPM. The Mustangs crossed the coastline at altitudes of 25-50 feet! Once they were over the continent, 270-275 KIAS and 2,600 RPM were the norm. The flight plans called for changing course every six minutes to make enemy interception more difficult. The Mustangs weaved constantly to thwart ground fire. Depressing the wing flaps a mere five degrees brought the nose of the aircraft down with little penalty in speed and facilitated the search for targets.

Mustangs attacked trains because a damaged locomotive on a single track disrupted traffic until the wreckage could be removed. If the engine exploded — tearing up the track and roadbed — so much the better. The pilots of Number 400 Squadron RAF claimed more than 100 locomotives destroyed

"The very early (Allison-powered) version of the Mustang was extremely fast. It was, I would say, at least as fast as even the late models. It began to lose power by the time you got to 5,000 feet. It was strictly a low-altitude aircraft.

We could outrun anything the Luftwaffe had. On more than one occasion we outran larger formations of aircraft — FW 190s or ME 109s. They could not keep up with the Mustang. The only thing that was faster than us was the Typhoon, and it had a much more powerful engine than we did.

We felt we had the best plane in the RAF for doing the job we were doing."
— Clyde East, Number 414 Squadron RAF

or damaged in their first six months of operation.

The Mustang's first air-to-air kill came on April 19, 1942, during the landing at Dieppe on the northwest coast of France. An American volunteer in the Royal Canadian Air Force (RCAF) flying in Number 414 Squadron RAF took down an FW 190. Ironically, the Mustang's pilot, Hollis H. Hills, was from Los Angeles, California — the birthplace of the Mustang.

In October 1942, a Mustang flew a reconnaissance mission over the Dortmund Ems Canal in northwest Germany, becoming the first RAF single-engine aircraft to fly over Germany in the course of World War II.

The Allison engines on early Mustangs were tough. The British routinely operated them beyond their recommended limits — full-throttle for as much as twenty minutes at a time without damage. The Allisons averaged 1,500 hours between bearing failures as compared to 500-600 hours for the Merlin. The Allison, they found, would drag them home even if the bearings were ruined.

The first two batches of Mustang Is ordered by the British — more than 620 aircraft in all — were direct orders. From the time they placed their third order until December 7, 1941, the British were supplied planes through lend-lease. Ultimately, 527 Mustangs were delivered to the RAF under lend-lease. When America was less than six months away from entering World War II, the British ordered an additional 150 Mustang IAs (NA-91). The only difference between this model and the Mustang I was that the eight machine guns were replaced by four 20-millimeter cannons. Ninety-three of the Mustang IAs from this first batch went to the RAF. When the Japanese attacked Pearl Harbor, the USAAF diverted a portion of this contract for conversion to the armed reconnaissance F-6A configuration. These were fitted with two F-24 oblique cameras. The F-6A became the first Mustang to serve with the USAAF — in the Twelfth Air Force, 68th Observation Group, 154th Observation Squadron in April 1943. The USAAF

lost its first Mustang to American ground fire during a strafing attack over Tunisia on April 23, 1943.

As the end of the production run of Mustang IAs for the British approached, General Henry "Hap" H. Arnold was made aware that NAA's substantial plant and skilled production line were about to go idle. Despite the disinterest initially exhibited by the USAAF procurement department, Arnold persevered and convinced them to order Mustangs. America's greatest strategic fighter of World War II entered mass production for its own country as an instrument for close-air support of infantry and armor.

"In North Africa the bomb release on an A-36A would not always free its bombs. A 3/8-inch spring was needed to provide the necessary extra kick. There were no springs in stock, but it was discovered that the springs under the saddle of a German motorcycle would do perfectly. Every captured motorcycle was stripped and springs supplied for A-36A bomb releases."
— AAF

P-51Bs at North American Aviation. In the foreground is a B-25.   USAFM

NAA began developing the A-36A, an attack/dive bomber version of the P-51A (Mustang I) in April 1942. The A-36A was armed with six .50-caliber machine guns (two in the fuselage and two in each wing) and was equipped with hydraulic above- and below-wing dive brakes and a rack under each wing for either a bomb (250, 300, or 500 pounds) or a drop-tank. A-36As featured a 1,325 horsepower Allison V-1710-87 (F-21R) engine, yielding a maximum speed of 310 MPH with two bombs at 5,000 feet. Without bombs, the A-36A reached 356 MPH. The first model flew the following September. The USAAF ordered 500 A-36A Invaders. The A-36A entered ser-

vice with the USAAF in April 1943, just prior to the invasion of Sicily.

The dive brakes reduced the dive speed from around 500 MPH to 390 MPH. The dive brakes tended to deploy asymmetrically, which was a serious problem. The result was an unstable dive, loss of control, and a fiery crash. Ground crews deactivated the dive brakes on many aircraft to prevent this problem. The loss of dive brakes, and the ferocity of German antiaircraft fire necessitated a reduction in the dive angle from the original 90 degrees to 70 degrees. The attack/pullout altitudes were increased from 8,000/2,000-4,000 feet to 10,000/4,000-5,000 feet.

The Mustang excelled as a ground support aircraft. The A-36As flew a total of 23,373 combat sorties and delivered more than 8,000 tons of bombs: they shot down 84 aircraft and took out another 17 on the ground. Losses due to enemy action totaled 177. The A-36A was well liked by those who flew it. The production of A-36As terminated in March 1943.

That same month, NAA began delivery of 310 P-51As. Fifty were delivered to the RAF as Mustang IIs. This shipment was to make up for the fifty-five Mustang IAs that the USAAF had retained for conversion to F-6As. Thirty-five P-51As were modified by the installation of F-24 cameras to become F-6Bs for the USAAF.

The P-51A's top speed was 390 MPH. The craft was armed with two .50-caliber machine guns in each wing. It was also fitted with wing shackles to carry either bombs or extra fuel tanks. Later P-51As were fitted with an improved Allison V-1710-81 (F20R) engine rated at 1,125 horsepower at 15,000 feet and 1,200 horsepower at takeoff.

Five P-51As were tested at the USAAF School of Applied Tactics at Orlando, Florida. In comparative tests and mock air combat exercises with its American contemporaries, the P-51A was found to have the best all-around fighting qualities of any American fighter below 22,000 feet.

The great transformation of the P-51 came at the hands of Rolls-Royce Limited. Four RAF Mustang Is (designated Mustang X) were handed over to Rolls-Royce for a trial installation of the Merlin 61 engine and a four-bladed airscrew. The Mustang X's propeller and gearbox were from Spitfires. Flight tests proved this aircraft capable of 441 MPH at 30,000 feet and of climbing to 20,000 feet in just 5.9 minutes (compared to the P-51A's 9.1 minutes).

North American redesigned the P-51 to handle the 1,520 horsepower Packard V-1650-3, a license-built Merlin 68 with a two-stage supercharger and an aftercooler. The airframe was strengthened to handle the new engine, the radiator installation was redesigned, new ailerons were fitted, and a pair of wing racks for long-range tanks or 500-pound bombs was installed. Later, the bomb load was increased to two 1,000-pound bombs.

General Arnold ordered 2,200 Merlin-powered P-51s for priority delivery. Seventy-one P-51Bs and twenty P-51Cs were converted to F-6Cs for photoreconnaissance. By summer 1943 the aircraft were in produc-

---

"We were a little reluctant about the P-51 the first time we saw it. It sounded like it was missing on all cylinders as it taxied up. We were used to the P-40, which had a fairly smooth-running engine. When you wound up the Merlin though, it smoothed right out. The Mustang turned out to be the best damn airplane for pilots and for crew chiefs. The engine was very reliable and easy to diagnose. The Merlin either ran great or it didn't run at all!"
—Ralph Annala, P-51 Crew chief, 337th Fighter Training Group, Sarasota, Florida

---

tion at Inglewood, California, (P-51B) and Dallas, Texas (P-51C).

On January 15, 1944, P-51Bs equipped with drop-tanks completed their first long-range mission as fighter escorts to Eighth Air Force bombers over Germany. The planes became available just in time. The Luftwaffe had been mauling the unescorted bombers of the Eighth. The bombers needed fighter escorts to press home their attack on the industrial heart of the Third Reich. The mission of strategic escort involved hundreds of people for each fighter that went aloft. Today, in a world of computer-driven spreadsheets and combat simulation programs, it is difficult to imagine the complexity of planning and executing even a single mission of this type.

Spring 1944 — 2245 hours:

The group S-2 intelligence duty officer (IO) glances at the yellow paper fresh off the teletype, signs the message, and retires. This is a warning order — an official tip that higher headquarters is considering a bomber escort to Erkner, Germany, a suburb of Berlin, the next morning. It is early; the plan may be changed numerous times before the fighters actually take off.

0100 HRS: The teletype operator rousts the IO and hands him another message — the field order. The show is on; the group will be escorting the bombers today. The IO rouses the duty operations officer. While you and the other pilots sleep, the IO and the duty operations officer begin the process of making plans for the group's part in the mission. The IO informs the group leader, the pilots, the engineering section, the weather officer, and all the other people involved in mission preparation.

The IO estimates the time for takeoff (0930 HRS) and works backward from that point to establish the briefing time (about one hour before engine start, which will be at 0920 HRS), mess hours (0730 HRS), rising time for the ground squadrons (0530 HRS or 0600 HRS), and rising time for pilots (0700 HRS).

The intelligence officers summarize the mission for presentation at the briefing. They describe the target, radio control, emergency facilities, expected enemy reaction, flak defenses, and position of ground troops, and try to outline the complete picture for the group leader.

A detailed map covers one entire wall in the briefing room. The red strings on the map represent the fighters' course — blue, the bombers'. The map shows your escort zone and possible strafing targets. A fighter plane silhouette with the number "78" is paired with a B-17 silhouette numbered "94." The Seventy-eighth Fighter Group will escort the Ninty-fourth Bomb Group on this mission. Tail and wing cutouts show the unit markings of the Ninty-fourth Bomb Group, a black square and white "A."

The mission timetable is displayed on a large board showing the time for engine start, takeoff, setting course, rendezvous, and so forth. This timetable must be followed to the minute if your group is to make its contribution to the mission.

As the S-2 officers finish the briefing boards, the squadron commanding officers (COs) are stirring from the orderly rooms and waking up the mechanics, armorers, radiomen, and others. The engineering and armament sections turn out.

Before they eat breakfast, two men for each ship, a mechanic and an armorer, hitch a ride on a truck or grab a bike to ride out to the waiting Mustangs. Other mechanics and armorers eat a quick breakfast in the mess and then relieve the others so they can eat.

Not many of the communications men are up. There are a few present to handle any unexpected problems. But since the radio section worked late last night, examining and testing transmitters and receivers after yesterday's mission, many of them are still sleeping.

Out on the line, your crew chief climbs into the cockpit as part of his pre-flight of the P-51 you will fly. He starts the engine and runs it up for a check. Meanwhile, the armorer is waiting his turn. When the propeller stops, the armorer opens the gun compartment on each wing and makes a quick visual exam of the .50-caliber machine guns, ammunition feed chutes, and cartridges. He reaches in and shakes each weapon to make sure it is securely mounted and will not jar loose while firing. Next, he charges the weapon, closes the compartment, and examines the gunsight.

As the crew chief and armorer finish up, the men who ate breakfast early arrive. Continuing flight preparations, the assistant crew chief prepares for the compressed oxygen suppliers and the fuel men who are already servicing nearby planes. Fuel tanks are topped

Eighth Air Force crew chief warms up a Mustang. USAFM

off and the oxygen bottles are filled for this high-altitude mission. A mechanic cleans off the canopy with a chamois, removing any smudge that might hide an attacking Luftwaffe fighter.

One mechanic stands waiting by your fighter. The rest wander off to their shacks to play cards or sleep.

The intelligence officers of Squadrons S-2 and S-3 continue to gather important

Armorer and his tools. USAFM

information, such as flak reports, to post on the briefing map. Operations clerks make last-minute contact with the ground echelon to determine which planes will be available for the mission, who will fly each one, and which aircraft have been put back in commission by the night-shift mechanics. Since missions are flown by day, maintenance and repair work

must be done at night. While you and the other pilots sleep, the airfield is alive with activity.

The engineering department says that twenty-four Mustangs from your squadron are good to go. The men of S-3 pass this information along to the briefer, then relax until it's time to take the pilots out to their fighters.

Squadron S-2 prepares course cards and maps for you. Accuracy is essential. A wrong compass bearing on a course card or an

"You had some prized possessions: like your specially tailored 'Ike Jacket' —it was a grand thing with the wings and bars all embroidered . . . not an issued item. You had your candy bar ration, your whiskey ration, and your eggs, which were bought from neighboring farmers. Everybody had a will—an oral will with a buddy. 'If I get it, you can have my eggs and my jacket.'"
—Dick Gross, 350th Fighter Squadron

A pilot runs up the Merlin engine of a P-51B. USAFM

error depicting the rendezvous point on a map could mean chaos in the air.

0700 HRS: Your last few minutes of sleep are disturbed by the sound of heavy bombers thundering overhead towards their formation assembly points. Before you leave the Nissen hut you share with nine other officers, you empty your pockets of any personal identification: wallet, notebook, latest letter from home. You slide into long johns and heavy socks, then put on olive drab wool trousers and a shirt with an Eighth Air Force insignia and a scarf. A heavy wool flying suit fits over all this. You double-check your "escape kit" — reichsmarks and francs, waterproof maps printed on linen cloth, concen-

---

"I still remember the checklist:
S C I G P T F R
Safety Belt Fastened
Controls Free
Instruments in the Green
Gas Full
Propeller Pitch
Throttle
Flaps
Runup"
—Dick Gross, 350th Fighter
Squadron

---

trated food rations, a couple of candy bars, and an extra clip of ammunition for your Colt .45. You stuff all this into your knee pockets, then sling on the shoulder holster with the heavy Colt. Lastly, you put on your leather A-2 flight jacket.

You reflect upon your "will." Who should get your whiskey and candy ration?

You and your squadron mates trudge off through the eternal mud to breakfast. Go easy on the liquids — this escort mission could last five or six hours.

0830 HRS: After a meal of powdered eggs, you and your squadron mates arrive at the briefing. The station weather officer steps to the front. All night, observers and forecasters have made regular readings of temperature, wind velocity, and barometric pressure. Combining this with data from other stations, the weather officer tells you what to expect in the way of clouds and winds at various altitudes along your route. He tells you at what altitude the contrail will appear, announcing your presence to the enemy below.

After the weatherman finishes, the mission leader takes over. Today the mission leader is your squadron CO. He is burdened with the weight of command; your group's successful participation in this mission is his responsibility. He points out the flak areas and enemy airfields you may have overlooked. You note the target, a ball bearings plant, and think

about how far a walk it will be to Denmark should you be unlucky.

At the end of the briefing you are issued your mission cards and maps. You head over to the personal equipment locker, where a sergeant signs over your parachute, collapsible dinghy, and the yellow orange Mae West life preserver. It takes only a few minutes to fly over the North Sea, but it would be a long, cold swim if you had to ditch or bail out. All of this equipment was inspected by the base personal equipment section and by squadron parachute riggers prior to pickup.

You toss your equipment in the back of a truck and ride out to your plane. Your airplane is a P-51B named *Jeane Rose*. You named this Mustang for your girlfriend back home in Cheyenne, Wyoming. The Jeane Rose you left at the Union Pacific train station is a brunette, but the artist who painted the nose of your craft made her a smashing redhead.

A mechanic helps you unload your gear and accompanies you on a brief walk around the plane. He tells you what repairs have been made and what might still be a problem. You check the tires, landing gear strut clearances, uncover the pitot tube, and check the caps on the gas tanks, the fuselage, the two wingtanks, and the two 108-gallon drop-tanks.

You can't get dressed for this party without help. The mechanic helps you with the Mae West. He snaps the parachute and dinghy together into a single unit and helps you put that on, too. When you're finished, you've gained about thirty pounds. You waddle about, stooping forward a bit to keep the dinghy from smacking you in the back of your thighs.

The mechanic climbs up on the wing and gives you a hand. You scramble up the left main gear tire and over the leading edge of the wing, past the drop-tank and the two open .50-caliber muzzles, and towards the cockpit. You throw one leg in and flop the dinghy into the seat, then drop down on top of it. The mechanic watches you closely as you plug in your oxygen hose, microphone, and headset.

The crew chief says a few final words: the usual admonition to bring the bird back in one piece.

It begins to drizzle lightly so you button up the canopy and wait for the signal to start. The mechanic jumps from the wing and stands off to the side, fire extinguisher in hand.

On a field with three squadrons of Mustangs and thousands of support personnel you are alone with your thoughts. You busy yourself by going through the engine start checklist: fuel mixture control at idle cutoff, propeller control full forward, throttle cracked open an inch, and fuselage tank selected.

0930 HRS: A flare goes up from the control tower.

You throw the battery switch on, clear the propeller, turn on the fuel booster pump, and hit the starter button. Four Hamilton Standard propeller blades march past and you switch on the ignition. With a clatter and bark from the short exhaust stacks, the engine fires up. You set the fuel-air mixture to normal and set the throttle at 1,300 RPM.

The crackling staccato of nearly eighty Merlin engines coming to life fills the air outside your fighter, but all you hear (and feel) is the rumble of your own machine.

Taxiing out there's no direct forward vision so you pop the canopy and, like everyone else, weave along the taxiway to the run-up area. The fighters line up abreast next to the runway.

You go over the pre-takeoff checklist: magneto check — 100 RPM right, 130 RPM left; run up the engine to 30 inches of manifold for one minute and make sure that coolant and oil temperatures stay within limits; test the mags again; check the propeller and the supercharger; set coolant and oil switches to AUTO-MATIC; set the mixture control to AUTO RICH and the propeller to full forward; set the throttle and propeller friction locks; flip the fuel booster switch on; confirm that hydraulic pressure is between 800 and 1,100 PSI with the engine ticking over at 2,300 RPM; secure the harnesses; scan the engine instruments, and confirm that the generator is charging.

Squadron of Mustangs warming up before a mission.   USAFM

Three squadrons share your airfield. Four pairs of P-51s have taken off before you. Across the field in a control tower, a corporal with binoculars calls out each plane's letter markings when the plane is airborne, and a private writes the plane's takeoff time on a chalkboard. You notice the crash truck and ambulance parked near the tower. You resolve they will not get any business today.

It's your turn. You release the brakes and turn into position on the runway. You close and lock the canopy. An enlisted man standing off your left wing waves a flag.

You draw the stick backward past neutral, locking the tail wheel. The elevator trim is set for takeoff at six degrees right rudder to counteract the tendency of the engine and propeller to pull your craft to the left. You release the brakes and deliberately, but smoothly, advance the throttle to yield 61 inches of manifold and 3,000 RPM. You and your leader begin to roll. By the time the engine hits 30 inches of manifold, it is making as much noise as it ever will, but the power just keeps coming. Nearly two thousand feet down the runway, you and your leader are aloft. The landing gear comes up, and the hydraulic pressure gradually returns to 1,000 PSI. You trim the nose down slightly and gradually reduce the rudder trim. You check your radios while you are still at a low altitude. There is no point in announcing the mission to the Germans. They will know

soon enough.

By the time your squadron CO has made one circuit of the airfield, the whole squadron is up. Two more turns around the field and all three squadrons are up and ready to head east. As the collective thunder of the formation dies away, the members of your ground crew pick up any scattered tools and equipment, then retire to their shacks for a well-deserved sleep. Sometimes, when sleep will not come, they play cards or talk.

The fighters form up in groups of four and begin the climb towards the rendezvous point. The weather today is pretty typical. You climb through 15,000 feet of murk. You drift the power back to 46 inches manifold and 2,700 RPM to give a climb air speed of 175 MPH. You scan the engine instruments and pressure gauges. Next you set the coolant doors to AUTOMATIC and turn the fuel booster pump to NORMAL. Then you set the super-charger to AUTOMATIC. You concentrate on the artificial horizon and air speed indicator while trying to keep your squadron mates in sight. At 10,000 feet you go on the oxygen that will sustain you in the cold, rarefied air over western Europe. Somewhere between 14,500 and 19,500 feet, the supercharger blower shifts into high speed. There is a momentary surge in manifold pressure and power until the regulator catches up. This is a big thrill when trying to maintain position in soup, since no two

P-51D on top of the clouds. USAFM

superchargers kick in at the same time. You have selected the fuselage tank, because you are trying to burn off at least half of the 85 gallons of gas behind you. Until this is done your Mustang is not a balanced gun platform; you cannot turn sharply without risking a stall, which is very difficult to recover from. When the fuselage tank reads a little less than half empty, you switch over to the drop-tanks.

0958 HRS: When you break out of the clouds, you're on top of the world. All around you, dozens of black specks emerge from the clouds, slicing through a cobalt sky towards the rendezvous point.

Over the Continent and still climbing, you spot the bomber stream. It is an incredible sight: the stream is nearly fifty miles long. There are hundreds of bombers, thousands of men, intent on destroying the same place: the

---

"Some guys got hit and couldn't control the airplane. One fellow had a shell explode in the cockpit which apparently tore his leg off. He talked all the way in — calmly."
— Dick Gross, 350th Fighter Squadron

---

ball bearing plant at Erkner, Germany. Cruising faster than the bombers, your group overtakes box after box of Fortresses until you reach the box with the distinctive black square and white "A."

One fighter group is assigned to cover each bomber combat box. Today, seventy-five Mustangs are tasked with covering twenty-one bombers. Your squadron is split into two sections to cover the left and right flanks of the combat box. A second squadron floats about 4,000 feet above the bombers. Finally, a third squadron flies in front of the bombers. You and your leader will fly the right flank.

Today the Luftwaffe attacks in force. While ME 109Gs fly top cover, the FW 190s attack head-on. There are five rows of Focke-Wulfs eight to ten abreast – a company front formation. From the radio chatter you learn that the forward squadron is fully engaged with a large gaggle of determined ME 109s. These FW 190s coming at you have slipped through.

1122 HRS: The radio crackles with the order to attack. You switch to an internal tank, punch the red button on top of the stick, and the tanks drop away with a brief plume of spilled fuel. You flick on the gun and camera switches. It has all come to this — the training and work of thousands of people have put you here, charged with a single responsibility: to protect the B-17s.

The combined closing rate of speed exceeds 500 MPH. The FW 190s are within range for only a few seconds as you jockey for a shot. You have to break up the attack in order to reduce the massed firepower bearing down upon the Fortresses. You and your leader open fire, getting hits simultaneously, but nothing decisive. The FW 190s jink to avoid your fire.

After the Focke -Wulfs make their first pass through the bomber formation, the aerial battle is no more organized than a barroom brawl. The neat divisions of Mustang squadrons dissolve into two-ship elements chasing down the enemy.

You bank left slightly and pop off some short bursts, aiming for a pair of FW 190s. When you see the flash of the .50-caliber

bullets tearing through the skin of the FW 190, you adjust your aim and hold the trigger down. The pair of Focke-Wulfs rips by, ducking below and behind.

Your leader pulls up into a loop. When he reaches the apex, you pick up the pair as they swing to your left. They turn, firing before you can level off. Your leader tells you to take the FW 190 on the right. You're on him, shooting from above. More hits. You're careful not to dive — at 26,000 feet you'd soon exceed your Mustang's maximum allowable air speed. The fighter would turn into a lead sled pointed earthward.

You twist into a punishing right turn just in time to see the pair whipping past and below you turning left. The g-forces pin you against your seat. You can hear your own ragged breathing through your headphone. You roll 180 degrees and pull the stick back until you can feel the buffet of an approaching high-speed stall. Back off !

The Germans are still spiraling downward, drawing you away from the bomber stream. You pick out the higher of the two fighters and try a shot. He's weaving back and forth and you're almost directly above him. Miss!

You tighten the turn, drop the flaps a notch, and fall in on his left rear quarter. He tightens his turn as you watch streams of vapor form off his wing tips. Your Mustang thumps through the German's prop wash. You're going too fast! You reef through your left turn to cut behind the Focke-Wulf and overshoot!

Now he's behind you. You pull the stick over and back, breaking hard right in time to see tracers flash past your left wing. Miss! He can't stay with you in the turn and falls away to your left.

Still swirling downward, he swims into your sights and you hit him hard. Bullet strikes twinkle across the right wing root and just forward of the cockpit. It's like watching a string of firecrackers explode in the dark. The wing snaps off and the FW 190 spins away like a firework gone berserk.

Your leader is closing in on the other

FW 190. You both slide into a quartering rear position and the hapless fighter disintegrates when struck by eight .50-caliber Brownings.

Suddenly, the two of you are alone. Scarcely three minutes have elapsed. You point your noses skyward and climb back toward the bomber stream.

There are no more close-in engagements today.

1240 HRS: Although your squadron was able to do a good job of protecting the bombers against the German fighters, you still have to watch helplessly as the B-17s plod through flak over the target. Most, but not all, get through to deliver their bombs.

The return is quiet. You and your leader form up on a straggler, a lone B-17G, marked with a black square and a white "J" tail identifier — 390th B.G. You don't approach from behind, the tail gunner might blast you. You just drift up on the left side and let them get a good long look at you. She is a little rough-looking. Engine four is down with the prop feathered. Engine three is running, but spew-

church steeple is a real possibility. On those days you hope the barometric pressure hasn't changed much since you left. No point in radioing for the current setting to calibrate your altimeter. The Germans will only too willingly give you a figure — the wrong figure.

1500 HRS: You pick out Great Yarmouth on the northeast coast of England and strike out for your home field. You keep picking up pairs of Mustangs as you wing closer to home. It looks like everyone is on hand for your return: crew chiefs and their assistants, armorers, radio men, fuel and oil men, flight chiefs from each section, flight surgeons, firemen, and medics. Everyone who sent you out is waiting, straining to hear the first faint snarl of the engines.

It would be a shame to get this far and mess up in front of such a huge audience, so you go through your pre-landing checklist. Select the fullest tank, turn the fuel booster pump to ON, select AUTO RICH on the fuel mixture control, set the propeller full forward, and tighten your harnesses.

Major James Goodson of the Fourth Fighter Group forms up with a B-17. USAFM

ing an evil-looking plume of oil smoke. You can almost see the grins on the pilot and the left waist gunner as you float into position next to the Fortress.

The descent today is not too bad. Sometimes the clouds are so thick that you have to fly so low that hitting a radio tower or

1525 HRS: Turning 2,700 RPM, you arrive over the field, scudding along at about 250 MPH. You and your leader slow to about 210 MPH and peel off. As the air speed dwindles to 170 MPH, you drop your landing gear. There's a double thump and a green light to confirm they're down and locked. You trim

away the nose down tendency, lay in half flaps, and trim up again.

As you turn onto the base leg you recheck the gear and flaps, making sure they're down, and watch the air speed drop to 140 MPH. The turn to final occurs about 250 feet over the ground and a quarter mile from the runway threshold. You lay in full flaps now and retrim again. When you're over the threshold at 120 MPH you ease the throttle back and let her float in nose high. There's the satisfying thump and rumble of a three-point landing.

You track down the runway until turning off onto the grass. You slide the canopy open, open both radiator doors, pull up the flaps, set the trim tabs to neutral, and switch off the fuel booster. You weave back to your tie-down spot and run through your last checklist. Set the propeller control to full forward, retard the throttle to 1,500 RPM, and set the fuel mixture to IDLE CUT-OFF. As the engine speed falls through 700 RPM, you advance the throttle and switch the battery and ignition to OFF. You pull out the hydraulic release handle between your legs, lock the controls, and turn all switches off. As the blades whistle down, you hear the other Mustangs arriving overhead.

With the engine shut down and still ticking as it cools, your mechanic and crew chief are up on the wings, rapidly firing questions: "Everything go okay?"; "Was the engine all right?"; "Any jams on the guns?" They help you out of the cockpit — you are clumsy after nearly six hours of sitting. The crew chief is satisfied that there are no bullet holes in "his" plane. Now he wants to know if "we" got any kills. You tell him that we got one FW 190 and half another. The plane performed perfectly, you say, and the chief grins broadly.

You dump your excess thirty pounds — the parachute, the dinghy, and the Mae West —and flop down in the back of the first vehicle that can take you to the locker and interrogation. Already, the gasoline and oil trucks are making their rounds. Camera specialists remove and replace the trigger-activated gun cameras in the wing root. The armorers begin cleaning the guns and changing any barrel that looks worn. Mechanics uncover the engine to look for oil and coolant leaks, check the tires, and pursue countless other details of routine scheduled maintenance. New drop-tanks are fitted and filled, and fresh ammunition is loaded into planes that need it. The radio men check the transmitters and receivers.

The engineering section looks at a plane in the adjoining revetment. A 20-millimeter cannon hit to the left wing needs attention. They will have to replace the wing. To escape, the pilot went to WAR EMERGENCY power. He notes this on the Form 1A. It looks like engineering will also have to replace the engine.

The squadron engineering sections then consult with the flight chiefs to determine which planes are due for routine inspection, which ones require minor overnight repairs, and which will take longer to repair. Squadron operations passes this information along to group operations. Group sends this information further upstairs. Upstairs will determine how many aircraft are available for tomorrow's mission.

At debriefing, you are queried about every facet of your flight. Was the weather as predicted? Were the German fighters showing any new or atypical markings? Did they attack from one direction, more than one direction? Were any multi-engine aircraft involved?

Two pilots report seeing something with two engines moving at an unholy velocity. Maybe it was an ME 410? The intelligence officer rolls his eyes and offers them another

whiskey. The intelligence officers gather the kill claims and other data for transmission to the group S-2 officer. He compiles a report for higher headquarters. Enlisted men collect your maps and file them away.

Three weeks later you will learn that the incredibly fast planes the two pilots saw are something called jets—Messerschmitt ME 262s.

You and your squadron mates scurry off to chow. You get to describe your air-to-air engagement again and again. It keeps unreeling in slow motion in your mind.

You are glad to be back. You turn in. Tonight you are lucky: sleep comes quickly.

Spring 1944 — 2245 hours.

Many pilots who did not survive a mission never saw their attacker. The blind spot behind the pilot in early versions of the P-51 was caused by the cockpit, which faired into the fuselage. This problem was corrected with the P-51D. The tenth production P-51B was fitted with a bubble canopy and the fuselage aft of the canopy was lowered for increased visibility. The P-51D first flew on November

Crash-landed P-51B.   USAFM

10, 1943. Armament was increased to six .50-caliber machine guns, all mounted in the wings. Later, in order to recover some lost directional stability, a small forward extension was added to the vertical stabilizer. The P-51Ds and P-51Ks were produced in greater numbers than any other Mustang models.

The P-51K's propeller differentiated it from the P-51D. The P-51 K was equipped with a hollow, steel, four-bladed Aeroproducts

propeller instead of the regular Hamilton-Standard unit. By the end of World War II, P-51D and P-51K models equipped more fighter squadrons in the USAAF than any other type of fighter.

The TF-51D, a variant of the P-51D, was the first fighter modified to give dual-instruction capability for transition, gunnery, and tactical training. The TF-51D was a two-place F-51D modified for pilot training per the request of the United States Air Force (USAF) Air Technical Service Command. Both the front and rear cockpits were equipped with all necessary flight instruments and controls. The landing gear could be extended from either cockpit, but could only be retracted from the front cockpit. Acceptance flight tests were conducted at the Texas Engineering and Manufacturing Company in Dallas, Texas, July 2-7, 1951. In level flight the larger canopy only caused an 8-10 KIAS loss in top speed.

During World War II American warplanes were, in comparison with their British and Japanese counterparts, heavy. In mock dogfights between a Mustang and a Spitfire, the Spitfire always prevailed. The Spitfire could outclimb, outaccelerate, and outmaneuver the P-51. In contrast, the P-51 could outrun and outdive the Spitfire. The Spitfire was a point defense interceptor designed to get aloft and perform over a small geographical area. The Mustang, on the other hand, was designed to cover some distance before engaging the enemy. The "B" models were equipped with an 85-gallon fuel tank placed behind the pilot for this purpose. With this tank full, the Mustang could not perform well in a dogfight.

In January 1943, North American began developing a lightweight Mustang variant, an interceptor along the lines of the Spitfire. The XP-51F was the first of three lightweight Mustang variants, all intended to fly long distances and to defeat any conceivable adversary.

The XP-51F was built using the British philosophy of limited load factors, simplified structures, smaller components, and new materials — plastic — in a calculated effort to minimize weight and maximize performance. North American had to make the Mustang leaner. The British had never bothered with calculating side loads on engines; their landing gear was designed to handle a 4G impact while the Americans insisted on 6G. The wings on American aircraft were marginally stronger and heavier.

The XP-51F was a complete redesign. No single structural part was interchangeable with earlier P-51 models. There was a new laminar flow wing section, the wings were thinner, the fuselage and radiator fairing contours were improved, and the engine mount and landing gear were lighter. The hydraulic system and cockpit layout were simplified. The craft's empty weight was reduced by nearly 1,600 pounds. Armament was cut back to four .50-caliber weapons. Internal fuel supply went from 269 gallons to 105 gallons. The XP-51F first flew on February 14, 1944, and subsequently reached a maximum speed of 491 MPH at 21,500 feet. NAA made three XP-51Fs for testing. The XP-51G and P-51J models were essentially "F" models with engine and propeller modifications.

The XP-51G — the next lightweight variant — was the fastest wartime Mustang. A five-bladed Rotol propeller coupled to a rare Merlin RM.14.SM engine (2,200 horsepower at 120 inches manifold pressure) propelled the XP-51G to 498 MPH. A second XP-51G with a Merlin 145 rated at 2,080 horsepower at 20,000 feet did 492 MPH at 20,700 feet and climbed to 20,000 feet in a mere 3.85 minutes. (The P-51A took slightly longer than 9 minutes to achieve this same altitude.) With its 105-gallon internal tank, the XP-51G could fly 510 miles at 315 MPH.

Strictly speaking, the last Allison engine Mustang variant was the XP-51J. The Allison V-1710 engine was fitted with a Merlin's supercharger system. The P-51J performed well, but with war's end, the need for it vanished. It first flew on April 23, 1945.

These three lightweights laid the foundation for the last production variant of the Mustang. A modified P-51F airframe was used

to make the first P-51H lightweight Mustang. The P-51H-1 first flew on February 3, 1945. The cockpit was redesigned, bringing the seat closer to the control stick in order to reduce fatigue on long-range missions. The P-51H was seven hundred pounds lighter than the P-51D. It also carried two fewer .50-caliber machine guns and was measurably quicker. The P-51H could do 487 MPH, climb 26 percent faster than the P-51D, and had a service ceiling of 41,200 feet. Three hundred seventy P-51Hs were produced by V-J Day. Production of Mustangs at Inglewood ceased on November 9, 1945, with the rollout of the 555th P-51H.

By this time, however, the frontline air forces of the world were equipping with jet fighters. By 1948 the P-51Hs were being turned over to Air National Guard (ANG) units in Indiana, Ohio, and Texas. During the Korean War call-up, P-51Ds from ANG units all over the United States were transferred into the regular USAF. P-51Hs stored at Kelly Field in Texas filled the void in ANG units. One is tempted to speculate how the P-51H might have fared against the jet-powered North Korean MIG-15s, but there were insufficient spare parts to sustain combat operations with the P-51H variants. The hottest production Mustang missed the opportunity to go against jets.

The P-51L was similar to the P-51H in all respects except the power plant. The P-51L was designed to use a Packard-built Merlin V-1650-11 engine featuring direct fuel injection, but none were ever built.

According to North American Aviation records, 15,486 Mustangs were manufactured at the Los Angeles and Dallas plants. Nine different production models were built. The Mustang bore the hallmarks of great design; it was an inexpensive, topnotch performer. The average unit cost for a Mustang in 1945 was $50,985, which compared very favorably with the Lockheed P-38 ($97,147) and the P-47 ($83,000).

Dutch Kindelberger and Lee Atwood went on to lead NAA into the jet age with the F-86 Sabre and the supersonic F-100 Super

Sabre, the first of the "century series" fighters. Dutch Kindelberger died on July 27, 1962.

Atwood succeeded Kindelberger, serving as president until 1969. By then, NAA had merged with Rockwell Standard Corporation to form the North American Rockwell Corporation. As of this writing, Atwood still lives in California.

Edgar Schmued, chief design engineer on the NA-73X project, died on June 1, 1985, in Oceanside, California. Fittingly, his ashes were flown out to sea in a P-51 Mustang.

It seems only through serendipity and the necessity of war that the Mustang ever came to serve the nation of its origin. The Mustang was built to British specifications and its full potential was finally realized by the addition of the Rolls-Royce Merlin. Though the Spitfire was a superior interceptor, the Mustang added range to the equation. As a strategic weapon, a fighter capable of taking the battle to the enemy, the Mustang was — if only for brief period—the perfect pursuit plane.

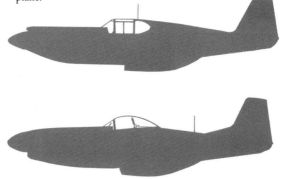

Previous page: Early versions of the Mustang had a razorback fuselage and a greenhouse canopy.   The P-51A is distinguished by the carburetor air intake atop the nose and the three-bladed propeller.   Bicycles were a common method of personal transport on sprawling air bases during WW II.

When the Mustang was fitted with the Rolls-Royce Merlin engine, a four-bladed propeller was chosen to convert the added power into thrust.   The bubble canopy was introduced with the P-51D version of the Mustang.   This modification resulted in a slightly lower maximum speed, but pilots felt the vast improvement in visibility was worth the sacrifice.

USAFM   USAFM

A

A   *The Mustang's conventional tail wheel configuration gives the fighter its trademark wide-shouldered stance. This wide track allowed for operations from grass airfields at forward bases as well as the paved runways of rear areas. The round object at the center is a light that swings down and illuminates when the gear is lowered. To the rear is the air scoop for the oil, engine coolant, and supercharger aftercooler radiators.*

B   *The P-51 vertical stabilizer is angled one degree to the right of fuselage's center line to counteract the torque created by a nearly 12-foot-diameter propeller coupled with a Merlin engine. The pilot had to add even more rudder; North American Aviation's flight manual states: "Before take-off . . . set rudder trim 5 degrees to the right."*

USAFM

Collection of Clyde East

B

A

PILOT CAPT. C.B. EAST
CREW CHIEF C.F. WARD
ASST. C. CHF. J.E. NASLUND
ARMORER E.R. PETERSON

AAF SPEC. PROJ. NO. 3121
U.S. ARMY F-6D-25NT
SERIAL NO. AAF 44-84786
CREW WEIGHT 200 LBS.
SERVICE THIS AIRPLANE WITH
GRADE 100/130 FUEL. T.O. 06-5-1 WILL BE
AVAILABLE T.O. 06-5-1 IF NOT
CONSULTED FOR EMERGENCY ACTION
SUITABLE FOR AROMATIC FUEL

SUITABLE FOR AROMATIC FUEL   HERE

5M

B

A   *In early versions of the Mustang the cockpit was enclosed by a segmented greenhouse canopy, which hinged on the fuselage and right side of the windscreen. The canopy folded inward and was secured by two latches. The razorback fuselage and canopy were designed to create the least amount of drag possible. Unfortunately, the configuration resulted in a blind spot behind the fighter. Some P-51B/C and F-6Cs were fitted with a backward-sliding bulged canopy that resembled the one on the Supermarine Spitfire. The bulged canopy was a theater modification; it did not change the aircraft designation.*

B   *The one-piece bubble canopy introduced with the P-51D allowed the pilot nearly unrestricted visibility and corrected the six o'clock blind spot of the earlier versions. The one-piece canopy is mounted on a metal frame that slides backwards past the seat, permitting cockpit access.*

C   *The ring and bead gunsight in this P-51A is typical of early World War II fighters in the Army Air Corps. The pilot had to make some large assumptions about deflection, drift, and the convergence of his guns.*

D   *The K-14 computing gunsight was a great improvement over the ring and bead. This precision instrument computed the deflection angles and diverging aircraft speeds as well as differing flight paths the pilot needed to keep his quarry inside a circle projected on the glass in his line of sight. According to the North American Aviation flight manual, "the gyro computes correctly only after the target has been correctly framed and tracked for a minimum period of one second."*

C

D

A

Previous page: The prototype Mustang and the early P-51 and P-51A versions were powered by the Allison engine. This power plant, also used in the P-40 and the P-38, performed superbly at low altitudes. However, it lacked the supercharger that allowed the Merlin engine to perform at high altitudes — which was essential in protecting bomber formations over Europe.

A   The engine of the P-51 was closely cowled to maintain the low-drag profile of the fuselage. The cowling panels were attached by DZUS fasteners for quick field removal by ground crews.

B   With a quarter turn, these DZUS fasteners would hold a panel tight at speeds above 400 MPH.

C   The P-51A mounted a three-bladed Curtiss Electric propeller.

USAFM

Previous page: The Rolls-Royce Merlin was an extraordinary engine, proven combat worthy in the Battle of Britain by RAF Hurricanes and Spitfires. When the Merlin engine was mated to the P-51 airframe, the full potential of the Mustang was realized. The Merlin, unlike the Allison, was fitted with a two-stage supercharger to maintain power at higher altitudes, where aerial combat was taking place over Europe. The four-bladed propeller was manufactured by Hamilton-Standard.

A   A seemingly endless supply of engines, airframes, ordnance, and spare parts allowed the Mustang pilot to push his machine to the limit. Operational fighter units replaced spark plugs between missions. If a pilot returned with a damaged engine, ground crews could replace it overnight.

B   An uncowled Rolls-Royce Merlin engine.

C   This manufacturer's plate is from a Packard-built Merlin, constructed under license in the United States to supply two separate P-51 Mustang production lines; one in Inglewood, California, and one in Dallas, Texas.

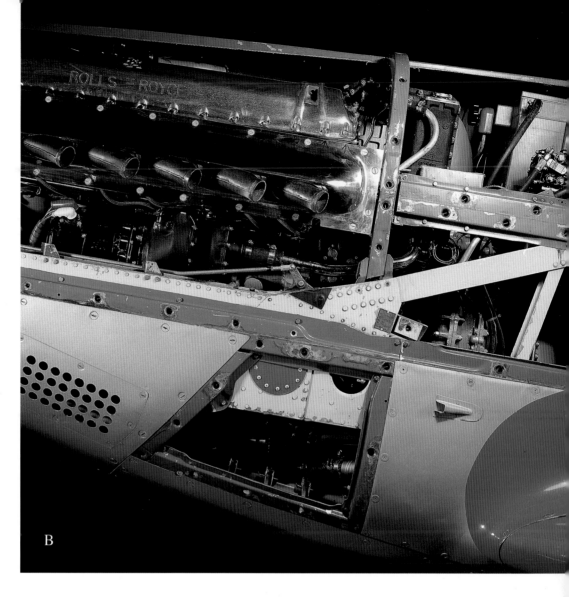

B

USAFM

C

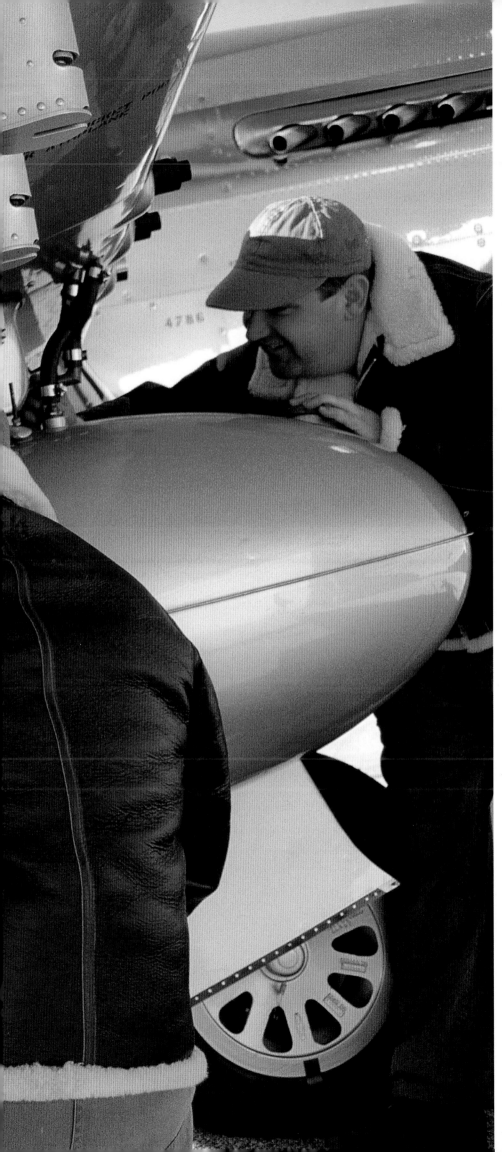

SERVICE THIS AIRPLANE
WITH GRADE 100 / 130
FUEL. IF NOT AVAILABLE
T.O. 06-5-1 WILL BE
CONSULTED FOR EMERGENCY
ACTION.

CAP. 75 U.S. GAL. 65 IMP. GAL.
SUITABLE FOR AROMATIC FUEL

B

A   Escalating losses of unescorted bombers were a critical problem for allied forces. The P-47 and Spitfire lacked the range to escort bombers all the way to a target. While it had better range, the P-38 was not an effective dogfighter at high altitude.   The Merlin-powered P-51, supplemented by underwing drop-tanks, was the solution to the escort problem.   The Mustang's aerodynamic design combined with careful fuel management allowed it to penetrate the farthest reaches of enemy territory.

B   The drop-tanks shown here are metal   75-gallon, pressurized tanks. Drop-tanks were also available in a 105-gallon size. Early in the war — before industrial production lines started — the British developed pressurized drop-tanks made from laminated paper. Tank pressurization was necessary to ensure a constant fuel flow as the fighter climbed to operational altitudes.

B

A   Ground crews included armorers who serviced the guns and underwing weapons carried by the Mustang. The P-51A had two .50-caliber machine guns in each wing. The gun bays, which store the ammunition, extend toward the wingtips. Each gun carried 400 rounds of ammunition, about 30 seconds of continuous fire. At lower left, wooden cases containing .50-caliber ammunition and spare gun barrels are shown.

USAFM

B   Armorers load the linked bullets into the tracks. Every fifth shell was a tracer marked with a red tip. The links come apart as the belts feed through the machine guns and the empty brass shell casings are ejected.

A   The P-51D carried six guns, three in each wing. The guns were placed in adjustable mounts that could be fine-tuned to direct a convergence of fire at a predetermined distance. The diagram on the inside of the panel shows the set-up positions for the guns at varying convergent distances.

B   The armorer's hands and tools of his trade.

C   Long ammunition bays fed the belts into the flexible tracks that led to the gun breeches. Early Mustangs had problems with guns jamming; this P-51D is equipped with the last wartime gun system developed for the fighter.

B

USAFM

C

43

A During stateside training, pilots making the transition from advanced trainers (North American AT-6s) to fighters often would start out in the early-model P-51A. In addition to gunnery training, pilots would have to solve navigation problems for long-distance flights, including flights over large expanses of water. This pilot wears lightweight flying clothes and a "Mae West" inflatable life preserver under his parachute harness.

B W.A.S.P. (Women's Airforce Service Pilots) volunteers transported P-51s and many other aircraft types from the factory to an acceptance point.

C The RAF operated the P-51A as the Mustang I and the P-51B as the Mustang II. The British, for whom the Mustang was originally designed, also mated the Mustang airframe with the Merlin engine. The result was the premier strategic fighter of World War II.

Collection of Clyde East

Collection of Clyde East

A

A   Cockpit of the P-51D Mustang. Top center: the K-14 gunsight. The padded cushion protects the pilot's forehead in case of a forced landing. Below, inside the white-lined box, are the primary flight instruments: the artificial horizon, gyro compass, altimeter, airspeed, turn and bank, and vertical speed indicator. To the right of the flight instruments are the engine instruments: manifold pressure, tachometer, carburetor temperature, oil, and fuel pressure gauges. Below the flight instruments are the fuel management controls. The control stick is full-forward, which unlocks the tail wheel for taxiing. To the pilot's right are the electrical switches; the handle and crank above those operate the canopy.

B   Ranging and sensitivity controls for the K-14 gunsight. The arc at center right has settings for various enemy aircraft. It is set for the aircraft of the Luftwaffe. Changing this setting enlarges or reduces the circle projected onto the glass in the pilot's line of sight. The pilot flew to the point where the enemy airplane spanned the diameter of the circle, the computing gunsight would make the calculations of deflection, and the pilot would pull the trigger. The red light in the circular housing at the upper left is the signal from the tail warning radar, a development that came very late in WW II. The light illuminated when an aircraft approached from the six o'clock position.

C   On the pilot's left, the throttle control is at top center. Pushing the handle forward increases engine power, which is measured by manifold pressure. The button on the end is the pilot's push-to-talk switch for radio communications. The round knob marked "P" is the propeller control, used to adjust the speed of the prop, which is measured by RPM.

The knob marked "M" is the fuel mixture control. It enables the pilot to enrich or lean the fuel-air mixture going to the engine. The trim controls, marked elevator, rudder, and aileron, are shown. The red handle forward of the trim controls is the landing gear handle; above it are the red handles that salvo the bombs.

USAFM

Collection of Clyde East

The pilot is ultimately responsible for the condition of the airplane he flies. Ground crewmen sometimes worked through the night in all types of weather to prepare a Mustang for its next mission, but the pilot must inspect the airplane to make certain that it is prepared to his satisfaction, since he will be the one flying at altitude, on oxygen, in combat.

A   A pilot reviews the condition of his fighter with the crew chief, who brings the pilot up to date on the status of the engine, armaments, fuel, and, in the case of the F6-D photoreconnaissance ship, the film and cameras. Here the pilot is inspecting the gun bays and ammunition tracks.

B   The pilot checks the control surfaces for undue play or stiffness — either problem could be fatal in a dogfight. He also checks the telescoping "oleo" on the main landing gear for the proper clearance. The tail and tail wheel were critically important assemblies.

C   Air intakes were checked for foreign objects.

D   A pilot's standard flight gear for a mission over Europe — a gabardine flight suit worn over the standard Class A uniform, with a leather A-2 flight jacket. Airmen flying over water were required to wear the yellow "Mae West" life preserver. The leather flight helmet is an RAF model, which many pilots preferred over the USAAF-issued helmet.

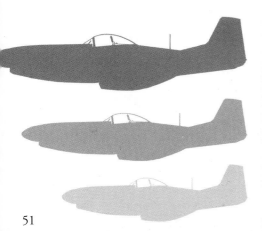

C

D

PILOT CAPT. C.B. EAST
CREW CHIEF C.F. WARD
ASST. C. CHF. J.E. NASLUND
ARMORER E.R. PETERSON

STEP HERE

A

A   Ground crewmen assist the pilot as he climbs into his fighter. The parachute is a standard seat type, which also served as the pilot's seat cushion. Some versions of this chute included a one-man inflatable dinghy. The back of the pilot's seat is armored with 3/4"-thick steel plate. Behind the seat are radio receivers and transmitters.

B   There was a strong sense of camaraderie among pilots and their ground crews despite the fact that the pilots were officers and ground crewmen were enlisted men. There was a mutual respect between men who flew and those who kept them flying. The British life preserver, helmet, and goggles are all standard RAF flight gear. The cold and damp climate of England made the fleece-lined jacket a necessity.

C   Between missions airmen took pictures to send home to the folks or the local press.

D   This pilot wears late-war flight gear. The A-2 jacket has been replaced by a fabric shell with a wool lining. Pilots got into the cockpit by stepping onto the main wheel and then up onto the wing.

Collection of Clyde East

53

A

A   Mission timetables included a period to warm up the Merlin engine properly. Pilots and ground crews used this time to bring the powerful engine to operating temperatures. Like any thoroughbred, the Mustang had to be treated carefully to realize its full potential.

B   Formation flying and constant radio contact with the unit did not change the fact that once he strapped himself into his cockpit and closed the canopy, the Mustang pilot was alone.

C   Before taking the runway, the pilot must perform a final systems check. The flight controls are moved through their entire travel, the Merlin engine is run up and checked for magneto operation, the propeller is run through a full range of RPM, the radios are set to proper frequencies, the rudder trim is set, the fuel selector is moved to the main tank, and the canopy is locked.

Next page : With the Merlin at full song, the Mustang takes off.

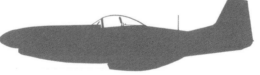

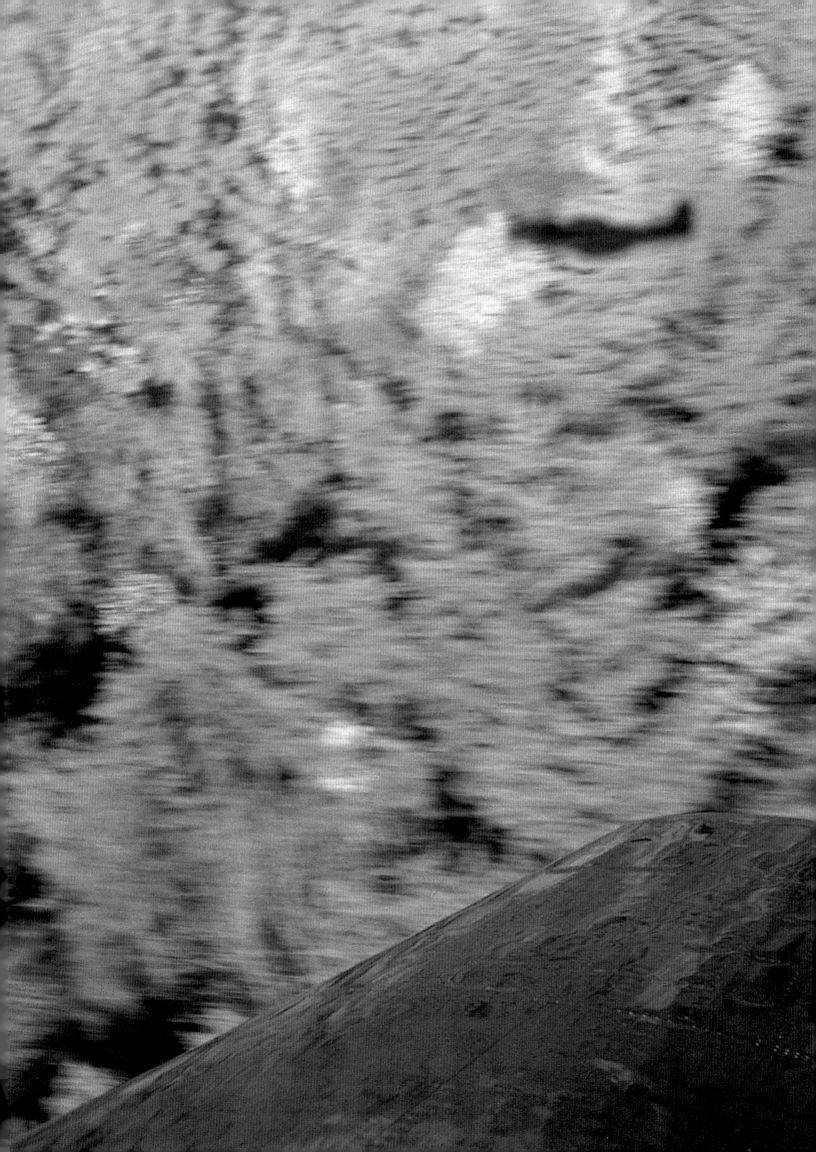

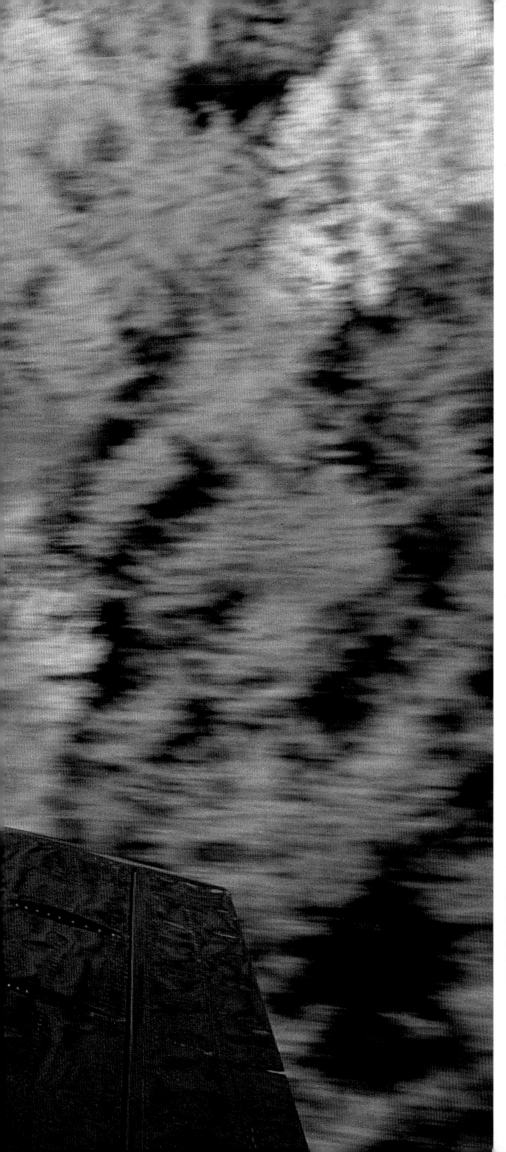

Fast and low — the Mustang's shadow is at the three o'clock position.

At one o'clock low another fighter . . . friend or foe?

USAFM

A   Looking to the twelve o'clock position, the P-51 flies at 250 MPH.

B   The pilot's hands are busy when flying the P-51; left hand on the throttle control, right hand on the stick. The wire gate ahead of the throttle marks the WAR EMERGENCY POWER selection. Shoving the throttle through this gate injected a water-methanol mixture into the fuel, maximizing engine output. Pilots were warned not to use this setting for longer than 5 minutes (an eternity in aerial combat). If the engine survived this use, it was usually replaced before the next mission.

C   Lil' Margaret over the trees. Pilots often flew photoreconnaissance missions at low altitudes to gain as much tactical detail as possible.

USAFM

A

A   The F6-D Mustang is distinguished by the camera ports just below and behind the national insignia. The lines and crosses on the left wing are reference points for the pilot during a photo run; they correspond to similar marks etched into the canopy. There was a third downward-pointing camera just in front of the tail wheel doors. The vertical low-altitude camera was patterned after those used to photograph the finish line at horse tracks.

Lt. George Goddard developed the low-altitude camera at the Dayton, Ohio, Wright Field photo lab. Film was transported through the camera towards the tail of the aircraft at a speed equivalent to the speed of the Mustang over the ground. The resulting photos looked like still photographs. In the summer of 1942, a P-51 fitted with this camera flew at an altitude of 200 feet at speeds of up to 400 MPH. In photographs that experiment produced, one could see the knotholes in a wooden bridge and the "A" on the gasoline ration sticker of a parked car.

B   The classic lines of the P-51 Mustang. On the undersides of the wings and above the drop tanks are the exit chutes where empty shell casings and ammuniton belt links were ejected during aerial combat.

C   The view of the six o'clock position. The bubble canopy of the P-51D provided life-saving visibility to the rear.

D Lil' Margaret on top.

Acknowledgments

This book would not have been possible without the help and cooperation of the following people. We owe them our thanks.

P-51D/F6-D *Lil' Margaret*

"Butch" Schroeder and Mike VadeBonCouer of Danville, Illinois. This Mustang was the Oshkosh 1993 Grand Champion World War II Award winner.

P-51A

"Moon" Spiller and David Spiller of Versailles, Ohio. This rare P-51 was rebuilt forty years after a crash in Alaska in 1943.

P-51D *Hurry Home Honey*

Charles Osborne, Brad Hood, and Andrea Lampen of Louisville, Kentucky. Mr. Osborne operates and maintains this beautifully restored fighter. It shares space with an F-4U Corsair and a P-47 Thunderbolt. Mr. Osborne hosts the Aviation Heritage Air Show near Louisville, which is always exciting to attend.

Dean Cutshall of Ft. Wayne, Indiana. Mr. Cutshall's Mustang was originally photographed for *Air & Space/Smithsonian* magazine.

The United States Air Force Museum, Col. Richard Uppstrom, USAF (Ret.), Director, Joe Ventolo, David Menard, and Bob Spaulding.

Rosann Patterson, my wife, and our kids, Nate, Brigitta, and Joe. When Dad goes to "play" with airplanes, they understand.

My lifelong friend, Paul Perkins.

Ross Howell and Howell Press.

Jeff Ethell for continuing to provide help and direction.

Clyde East, 414 Tactical Reconnaissance Squadron, RCAF, Fifteenth Tactical Reconnaissance Squadron, Ninth Air Force, Dick Gross, 350th Fighter Squadron, 353rd Fighter Group, Eighth Air Force, and Air Vice Marshal Ron Dick, RAF (Ret.), for insight into the actual flying of a Mustang.

Ralph Annala, P-51 Crew Chief, 337th Fighter Training Group, for insight into how to keep a Mustang flying.

I would also like to thank Rob Barnes, Tom Whalen, Dave Timmons, Rich Grumbley, David Hake, Mia Kosicki, and the late Dutch Biel.

The men and women pictured in this book represent organizations that are dedicated to preserving the uniforms and remembrances of World War II veterans. These groups provide historically accurate crewmen and women for airshows across the country. These individuals come from separate associations with a common goal, to get the facts right and communicate them to lay people. The help and advice they provide are invaluable, and I owe them many thanks.

Dave Berry, Dale Burrier, Hugh Daly, Ted Filer, Tom Horton, Peggy Horton, Tom Kosicki, Rob Millard, Troy Mulvaine, Shelly Mulvaine, Tim Thompson, Kurt Weidner, and Bruce Zigler participated in the P-51A photography.

Todd Guthrie, Dave Mattson, and Alan Winfrey took part in the P-51D/F-6D *Lil' Margaret* photography.

Troy Mulvaine took part in the P-51D *Hurry Home Honey* photography.

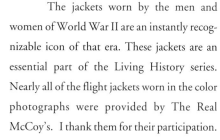

The jackets worn by the men and women of World War II are an instantly recognizable icon of that era. These jackets are an essential part of the Living History series. Nearly all of the flight jackets worn in the color photographs were provided by The Real McCoy's. I thank them for their participation.

The Real McCoy's is not a brand name. It is a symbol for flight jacket collectors. If you have a desire for the sky, a longing for adventure, or a reverence for past heroes, then you are already a comrade of The Real McCoy's.

"The Real McCoy's for the ultimate seeker"

For more information:

The Real McCoy's
66 Fitzgerald Avenue
Christchurch, New Zealand
Telephone 1-64 3 377 1017
FAX   1-64 3 366 6275

Technical Notes

The original photography in this book was all done with the intent to as faithfully as possible remove the clues of the present day and try to look back through a window opened by the owners and operators of these aircraft, a window into the 1940s when formations of these airplanes flew over the European continent during World War II.

I used a variety of cameras and equipment to complete this project: a Wista 4x5 Field View camera with a 150mm Caltar II lens and a 90mm Nikkor lens; a Mamiya RB67 with 50mm, 90mm, and 180mm lenses; and a Nikon F3 with a motor drive and a garden variety of Nikkor lenses.

All the photographs were shot as transparencies to make the best possible color separations.

The 4x5 and 6x7 photos were all shot on Kodak Ektachrome Daylight film. The 35mm photos were all taken with Kodachrome 200.

The concept, design, and the photographs are done by Dan Patterson, 6825 Peters Pike, Dayton, Ohio 45414.

Bibliography

BOOKS:

AAF: Official World War II Guide to the Army Air Forces. New York: Bonanza Books, 1988.

Angelucci, Enzo. *The American Fighter: The Definitive Guide to American Fighter Aircraft from 1917 to the Present.* New York: Orion Books, 1987.

Bowman, Martin W. *Castles in the Air: The Story of the B-17 Flying Fortress Crews of the U.S. 8th Air Force.* England: Patrick Stephens Ltd., 1984.

Caldwell, Donald L. *JG 26: Top Guns of the Luftwaffe.* New York: Ivy Books, 1991.

Carson, Leonard. *Pursue and Destroy.* Granada Hills, CA: Sentry Books, Inc., 1978.

Duxford Diary. Cambridge : W. Heffer & Sons Limited, 1945.

Ethell, Jeffrey L. *Mustang: A Documentary History of the P-51.* New York: Jane's Publishing Co. Ltd., 1981.

Ethell, Jeffrey L. et al. *The Great Book of World War II Airplanes.* New York: Bonanza Books, 1984.

Freeman, Roger A. *Mustang at War.* Garden City, NY: Doubleday & Company, 1974.

Harry, G.P., ed. *339th Fighter Group.* Paducah, KY: Turner Publishing Company, 1991.

Heiman, Grover. *Aerial Photography: The Story of Aerial Mapping and Reconnaissance.* New York: Macmillan Company, 1972.

Higham, Robin and Siddal, Abigail T., eds. *Flying Combat Aircraft of the USAAF-USAF.* Ames, IA: Iowa State University Press, 1975.

History of the 364th Fighter Group. Marceline, MO: Walsworth Publishing Co., 1991.

Infield, Glenn B. *Unarmed and Unafraid.* London: The MacMillan Company, Collier-Macmillan Ltd., 1970.

Jane's Fighting Aircraft of World War II. New York: Military Press, 1989.

Lande, D.A. *From Somewhere in England.* Osceola, WI: Motorbooks International Publishers & Wholesalers, 1991.

Leary, Penn, ed. *Test Flying at Old Wright Field.* Omaha, NE: Westchester House Publishers, 1991.

Pilot Training Manual for the P-51 Mustang: AAF Manual 51-127-5. Washington, DC: Headquarters Army Air Forces, 1945.

Rust, Kenn C. *Ninth Air Force Story.* Temple City, CA: Historical Aviation Album Publications, 1982.

Stanley, Roy M. *World War II Photo Intelligence.* New York: Charles Scribner's Sons, 1981.

Wagner, Ray. *Mustang Designer: Edgar Schmued and the Development of the P-51.* New York: Orion Books, 1990.

PERIODICALS:

Dick, Ron. "Meet the Mustang." *Air & Space/Smithsonian,* June/July 1991.

Dan Patterson is a self-employed photographer, graphic designer and private pilot living in Dayton, Ohio. Previous books are *Shoo Shoo Baby, A Lucky Lady of the Sky* , *The Lady: Boeing B-17 Flying Fortress,* and *The Soldier: Consolidated B-24 Liberator.*

Paul Perkins is an emergency room physician living in Yellow Springs, Ohio. Previous books are *The Lady: Boeing B-17 Flying Fortress* and *The Soldier: Consolidated B-24 Liberator.*